# MUSIC THEORY

# THROUGH LITERATURE

## VOLUME I
## WORKBOOK

# MUSIC THEORY THROUGH LITERATURE

## VOLUME I
## WORKBOOK

### John Baur

*Memphis State University*

PRENTICE-HALL, INC. *Englewood Cliffs, New Jersey 07632*

Editorial/production supervision and interior design: Dan Mausner
Cover Design: 20/20 Services, Inc.
Manufacturing buyer: Ray Keating

Printed in the United States of America
10  9  8  7  6  5  4  3  2  1

0-13-607839-7    01

Prentice-Hall International, Inc., *London*
Prentice-Hall of Australia Pty. Limited, *Sydney*
Editora Prentice-Hall do Brasil, Ltda., *Rio de Janeiro*
Prentice-Hall Canada Inc., *Toronto*
Prentice-Hall of India Private Limited, *New Delhi*
Prentice-Hall of Japan, Inc., *Tokyo*
Prentice-Hall of Southeast Asia Pte. Ltd., *Singapore*
Whitehall Books Limited, *Wellington, New Zealand*

# Contents

# Preface

The workbooks to Music Theory Through Literature have been designed to supplement the text in several important ways. Although limitations of space and format prevented extensive exercises in the main text, these expansions could be accommodated in the workbooks. In most chapters there is an attempt, as in the main text, to present technical skill exercises in addition to more creative projects. Both types are important, but for different reasons, and they should be mixed in a way most comfortable for the instructor, considering the needs of the specific class. Whenever possible there has been an effort to include actual musical examples from the period under discussion. In some cases both creative and skill factors have been superimposed through the use of excerpts from a composer's work.

There are several review sections placed strategically throughout the book, approximately every four or five chapters. These contain both written material—sometimes with one-word answers, sometimes in fully expository style—as well as musical examples from various styles.

Because space was less of a problem in the workbooks, there are more complete pieces than in the main text. It is hoped that such additional analytical exercises along with the written reinforcements, will strengthen the student's grasp of musical style concepts.

It should be pointed out that, as a general rule, there are more exercises than can normally be assigned. It is hoped, therefore, that the teacher will vary the choice of materials throughout the volume, providing the student with both breadth and flexibility.

J.B.

# Gregorian Chant and Secular Monophony

1. The following chant melody was composed by the process of centonization. Study the seven melodic motives found in this mode (given below) and trace their use in the melody. Be careful to notice any alterations of the motives which the composer has made. What is the mode?

LU 1360

mi — no    Si - cut    Glo — ri - a    Pa — tri    et    Fi - li —

o    et    Spi — ri — tu - i    San — cto    Si - cut

Melodic motives from which the chant was constructed*

a.

b.

c.

d.

e.

f.

g.

* From Willi Apel, *Gregorian Chant*, (Bloomington, Ind.: Indiana Univ. Press, 1958) p. 333.

2. Identify the mode of each chant fragment. Provide a brief reason for your choice of mode.

mode: _____
reason:

mode: _____
reason:

mode: _____
reason:

mode: _____
reason:

mode: _____
reason:

mode: _____
reason:

3. Study the following chant melody. Mark the recurrent motives. Identify the mode. What intervals are used?

LU 22  (Kyrie Deus sempiterne)

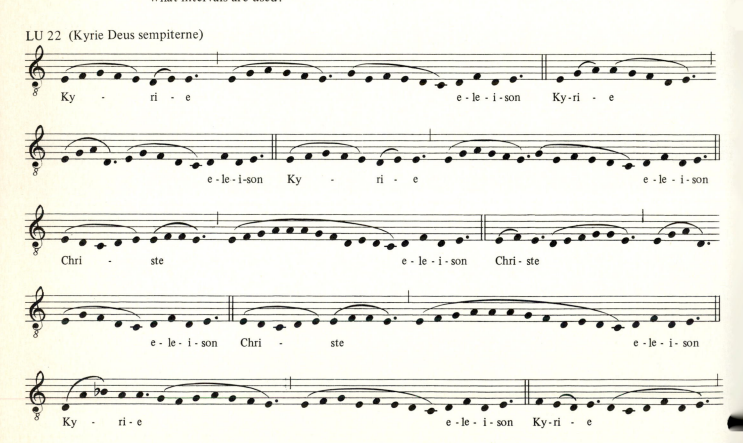

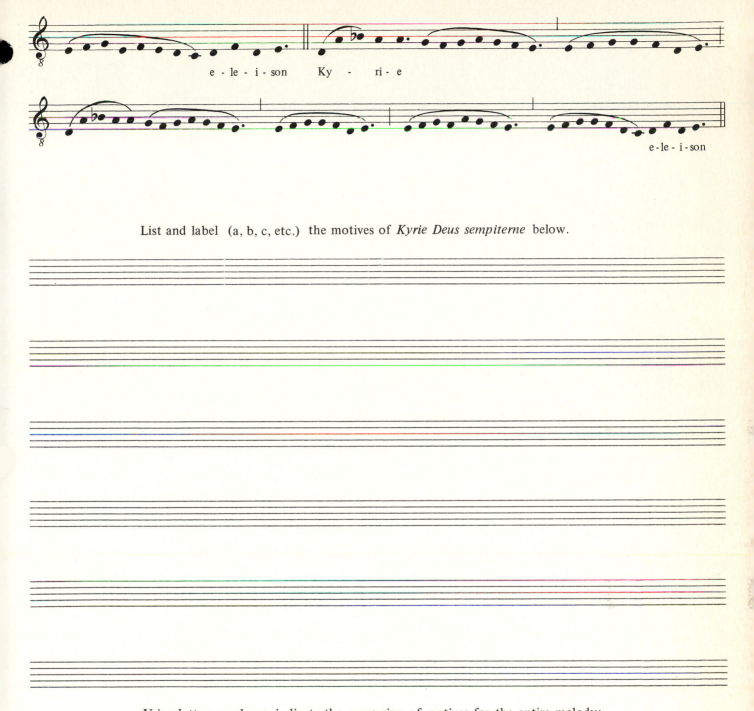

e - le - i - son    Ky - ri - e

e - le - i - son

List and label  (a, b, c, etc.)  the motives of *Kyrie Deus sempiterne* below.

Using letters as above, indicate the succession of motives for the entire melody:

4. Compare the following three examples of secular monophony for the use of scale and mode, phrase structure (length and shape), rhythmic mode (and rhythm in general), and overall form.

a.

Quant voi le felon
Perrin d'Angicourt

©Copyright 1960 Arno Volk Cologne

b.

Ce fu en mai
Moniot d'Arras

©Copyright 1960 Arno Volk Cologne

Dansa
Giraut d'Espanha de Toloza

c.

1. Ben vol - gra, s'es - ser po - ges,   C'A - mors si gar - des d'ay - tan,   Que non

fe - ses fin ay - man   Chau - sir en luec quel pla - ges.   E per que? Car
2. A - mors vos mi
3. E ten - ray m'ab

1. per pla - zer   Qu'ieu cre - sia de vos a - ver.   Don - na, vos mi fes chau -
2. fes a - mar   E chau - sir vos - tre cor car   E vos - tra beu - tat pla -
3. des - a - mor   Et au - ray gauch e so - cor   E jay e pla - ser en -

1. sir   A - mors, don a - via es per   Que mi de - ges - ses va - ler   Del joy
2. sen   Per pla - ser; mas gens an - car   Non ay mas dol e pen - sar,   E non
3. tier.   E qui si vull' aj' a - mor!   Qu'el viu - ra ab gran do - lor   Et ieu

1. don ieu tan sos - pir.   Ar m'a - ves a tal punch mes,   Que tot jorn vauc
2. truep nul ga - ri - men.   E pos per pla - ser ay pres   Pe - na, do - lor
3. ab gran a - le - grier.   E si d'ays - so suy re - pres,   Sap - cha ma ra -

1. de - si - ran   La mort, don ay do - lor gran;   Car non faitz so c'a - mors fes.
2. et af - fan,   A - mors me - ti a mon dan,   Qu'a re - bu - san a pa - les.
3. son e - nan:   C'A - mors van con - tra - ri - an,   Per so ayl con - tra - ri pres.

4. Mon de - liech, non vos vuell ges,   Mas mon des - pla - ser de - man;   E si as el
5. E mal an, pues qu'es - ser m'es,   Qui A - mors ser - vi - ra tan,   Con a fah, de
6. DAN - SA car ieu ay a - pres   Que-l Reys Kar - les fay gent chan,   Per a quo as

4. mi co - man,   leu au - ray tot cant obs m'es.
5. say e - nan;   Car non fan so que dretz es.
6. el ti man;   Car de fin pres es a - pres.   7. Ben vol - gra, s'es - ser po - ges,

C'A - mors si gar - des d'ay - tan   Que non fe - ses fin ay - man   Chau - sir en luec quel pla - ges.

**mode**

    a:

    b:

    c:

**phrase structure**

    a:

    b:

    c:

**rhythmic mode (predominant)**

    a:

    b:

    c:

Briefly discuss the differences in rhythmic use in each.

**overall form** (Indicate sections by capital letters—A, B, C, etc. Where sections are repeated with slight alteration indicate thus:  B B')

    a:

    b:

    c:

# 2

# Polyphony of the 10th, 11th, and 12th Centuries

1. Sing and play each of the following examples. Analyze each harmonic interval, paying special attention to the interval used at the beginning and ending of each word.

a. free organum (School of Winchester)

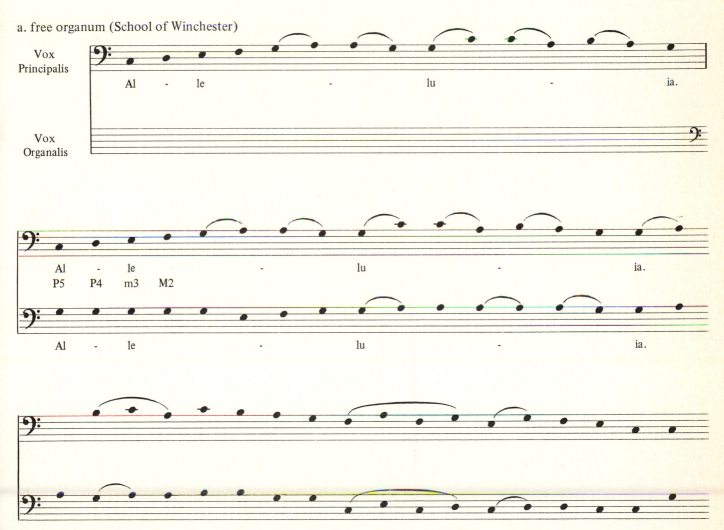

### b. melismatic organum (School of St. Martial)

Que          cor          -          da no          -
Ex    -    pul          -          sis in

stra          si - bi    fa          -
de          cunc - tis    vi          -

ci    -    at          ha - bi          -
ti    -    is          spi - ri          -

ta    cu    -    lum,
ta - li    -    bus.

©1962 Arno Volk Cologne.

c.

### Notre Dame Organum

m7 P8 —    — m7 P8 M2 —    P8          M2

Gau                                        de

Ma

ri

a.

2. Complete this example of free organum, using note-against-note style and primarily perfect consonances throughout.

3. Complete this example of melismatic organum. The chant is given in its entirety above the organum example. Construct the upper voice (vox organalis) in a melodic, singing style, beginning and ending each phrase with a consonance.

(Benedicamus Domino)

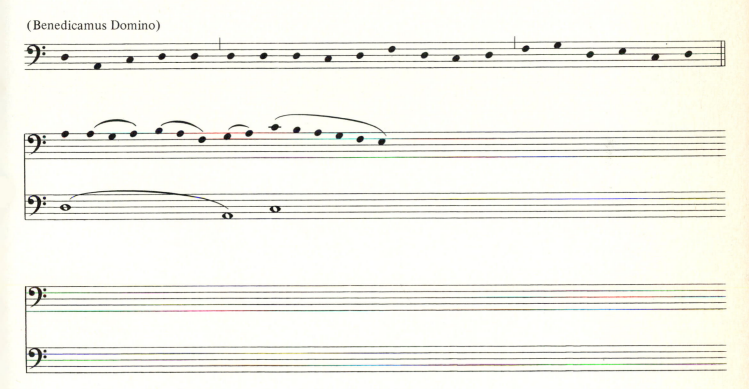

# 13th Century Polyphony

1. Analyze the harmonic intervals in the following example from the Montpellier Codex. Note the prominent use of perfect consonances.

Lonc tens ai mon cuer as-sis en bien a-mer, kon-ques vers a-mours ne fis riens

In seculum
P5   m6  P5

a blau-mer, ainz me sui mont en-tre-mis de lui lo-er. Or he puis mes

en-du-rer, si m'a con-quis de sa ioi-e m'a si pris, n'i puis du-rer.

iterum

© 1962 Arno Volk Cologne

par    mi    sunt    si    pleur et    si    ris,    tout truis    a - mer    quant    le    quit meil - lor    tro -

ver,    lors    me    fet    pis    dieus!    quant    ie    me    doi

la    nuit    re - po - ser,    res - veil - lent    moi    li    doz    mal    d'a    -    mer.

2. Write modal cadences in three voices, ending on the pitches indicated.

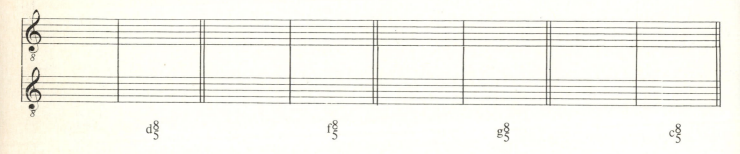

d$^8_5$    f$^8_5$    g$^8_5$    c$^8_5$

3. Complete the two upper parts of each motet fragment, ending the piece with a double-leading-tone cadence. The middle voice in the last example should be the lowest voice at the cadence.

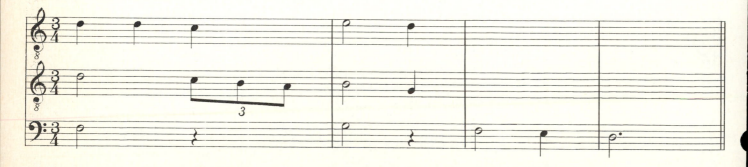

3

4. The beginning of a motet from the Bamberg Codex is shown below. Given the complete tenor and the harmonic intervals and roots, complete it in similar style. Use occasional passing tones and neighboring tones. At the rests in the tenor line, continue one or both of the upper lines, as in measures two and four.

5. Circle and label the dissonant pitches in the following example by Adam de la Halle.

# 4

# 14th Century Polyphony

1. Below is given the opening of a Machaut motet. Carefully analyze the use of
   isorhythm. Consider the rhythmic construction of the upper two voices and their
   relation to the tenor. Complete the final talea of the piece, with a one-measure
   extension for a modal cadence at the end.

Fera pessima

2. Identify the following cadences as to type (double-leading-tone or Phrygian).

3. For the following two fourteenth-century pieces, identify the basic compositional techniques used. Bracket each cadence and identify it. In addition, analyze the harmonic structure of the first example.

Philippe de Vitry

Triplum

Motetus

Tenor

Tu -

In

Virgo sum. Tenor. Nigre notule sunt imperfecte et rube sunt perfecte.

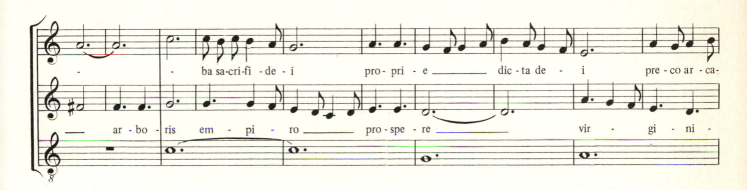

- ba sa-cri-fi -de - i    pro - pri - e _____ dic - ta de - i    pre - co ar-ca-

_____ ar-bo - ris em - pi - ro _____ pro-spe - re _____    vir - gi - ni -

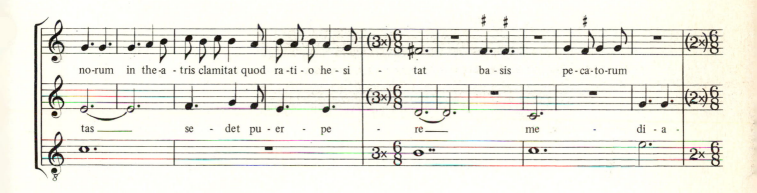

no-rum in the-a -tris clamitat quod ra -ti-o he-si    - tat    ba-sis    pe-ca-to-rum

tas _____    se - det pu-er - pe    re _____    me    di - a-

fa - tendum simpli - ci - ter _____    cre-den dum-que fir - mi - ter _____    mo - ri - ve

trix _____    fi - des _____ In _____ me - di - o _____

-na-tu-ra-li - a i - sta cum sint om-ni - a cre - den - ti - bus vi - ta ne - cis ne - gli-

dum _____ ma - gis ni - ti - tur _____

- gen - ti-bus na-tu - re quod gres si - bus ra - ti-o po - ti - ta in _____ pre - mis sis du - bi-

de - bi - li - tas _____ ra -

- um gi - gnat et au - gu - ri - um i - gi - tur ni-te-tur et ____ fi - des per quam ____ vi

- mo - rum fran - gi - tur _____ Pe - tat er - go ____ fi-de-

- a a - pud ar - cha-na-di - a cla - ri -or ha - be-tur sem-per i - mi-te-tur.

- i dex - te - ram vel e - ter-num ni - te - tur per - pe - ram.

# General Review: Chapters 1–4

I. Briefly answer the following questions.

1. What cadence is found most often in the late thirteenth and fourteenth centuries? _____

2. Define precisely the types of chord and interval structure used in this thirteenth to fourteenth century cadence. _____ _____

3. What is the name of the section of Notre Dame organum in which the tenor is notated in faster values? _____

4. What is the earliest and simplest type of organum? _____

5. What is the Latin name of the voice which uses the plainchant? _____
   The voice which is added to the chant? _____

6. What are the names of the three voices in a late-thirteenth or early-fourteenth-century motet? _____ _____ _____

7. From what type of piece did the motet derive? _____

8. What are the most prominent interval structures found in late-thirteenth-century (Petrus de Cruce) motets? _____ , _____ , _____

9. What is the name of the process of constructing a new chant melody from fragments of pre-existing chants? _____

10. Which intervals are termed consonances? _____ imperfect consonances? _____ dissonances? _____

11. What is the range of a mode called? _____

12. A mode is defined by its _____ , _____ and _____ .

13. Music which consists only of one line is termed _____ .

14. Music composed of several independent lines is called _____ .

15. Chant which has only one note per syllable of text is referred to as _____ . a few notes per syllable? _____ many notes per syllable? _____

16. How many rhythmic modes are there? _____

17. List the Greek names of the eight church modes, and indicate the final of each.

    mode 1:

    mode 2:

    mode 3:

    mode 4:

    mode 5:

    mode 6:

    mode 7:

    mode 8:

18. In a two-voice composition, if one voice moves while the other remains stationary, what is the relative motion called? _____

19. If both voices of a two-voice piece move in opposite directions, the relative motion is called _____ .

20. If two voices move the same distance in the same direction the relative motion is called _____ .

21. What is a dissonance called if it is approached and left by step in the same direction? _____

22. The repetitive melodic pattern in isorhythm is called _____ .

23. The repetitive rhythmic pattern in isorhythm is called _____ .

24. What does the expression D$\frac{8}{5}$ mean? _____

25. If each of the three voices in a motet use a fixed, repeated rhythm, what term would describe it? _____

26. What is the only type of organum which uses notated rhythm? _____

27. In what voice of a motet is the borrowed chant found? _____

28. What is the most prominent root movement found in Machaut's motets? _____

29. If the voices of a composition are written one after another, the process is called _____ .

30. If a melodic line is broken up and performed by two alternating voices, the technique is called _____ .

31. What is the name given to the period of music beginning with the early fourteenth century? _____ the twelfth–thirteenth centuries? _____

32. The technique by which rhythmic values are halved is called _____ .

33. Occasionally accidentals are added to a piece where the composer did not indicate them. What are these called? _____ _____

34. If the lowest voice of a motet cadences by moving down a half step, the cadence is called _____ .

II. Answer the following questions in discursive style, using the space provided.

1. Describe the difference between a double-leading-tone cadence and a Phrygian cadence.

2. Define the musical characteristics of the early fourteenth century, and in particular Machaut.

melody:

rhythm:

harmony:

dissonance:

cadences:

techniques:

3. What are the primary differences between thirteenth and fourteenth-century motets? The similarities?

4. List and describe the four types of organum.

III.  Analyze the short excerpts as directed.

1. Indicate in one or two words what musical technique is being used in each excerpt.

a.

technique: _____

b.

technique: _____

c.

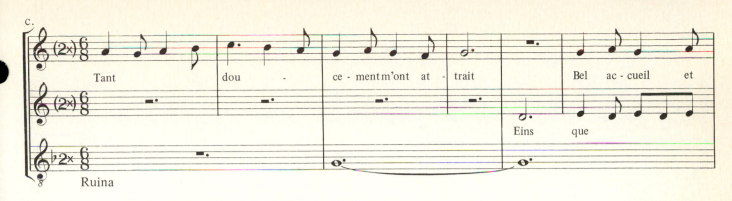

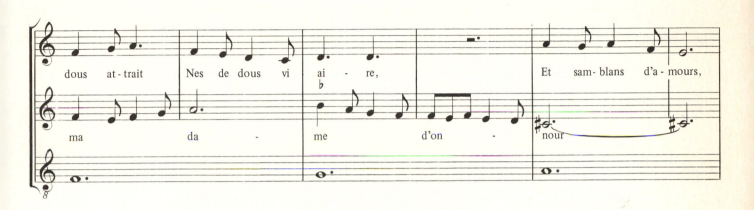

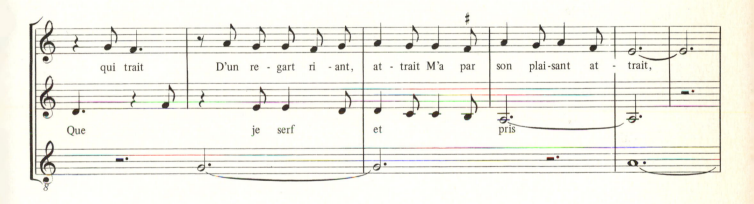

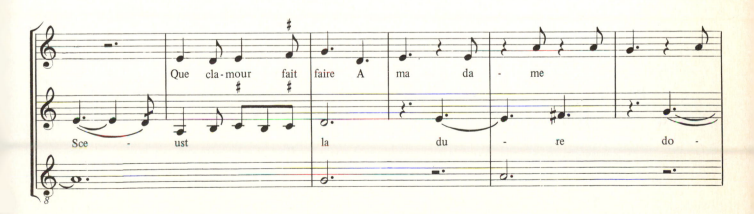

technique: _____

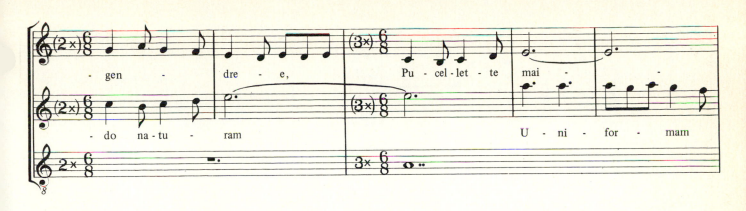

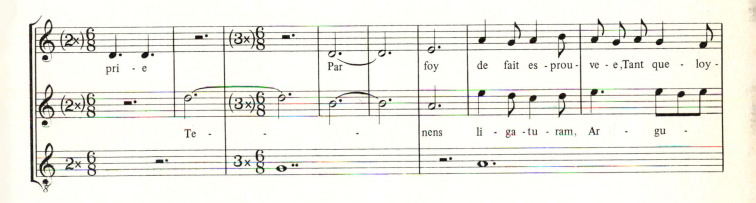

technique: _____

technique: _____

technique: _____

2.    Identify the following cadences.

_____    _____

_____    _____

3. Label the dissonant pitches in the following excerpt.

derived from Machaut

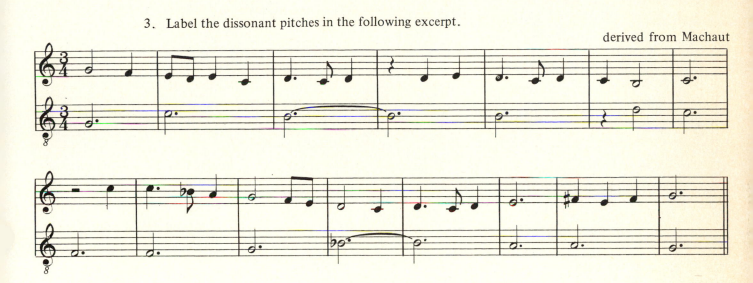

# Early 15th Century Polyphony

1. Write an upper voice over the given bass line. Include passing tones, suspensions, and escape tones as indicated. Include an under-third at one or more cadences.

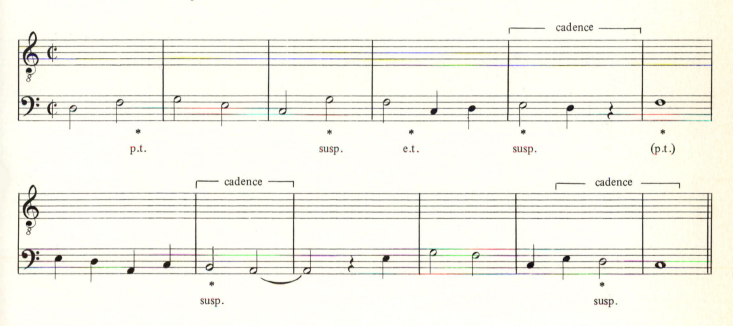

2. Identify the following cadences.

3.  Below is given the *Alma Redemptoris Mater* by John Dunstable. Provide a detailed analysis of the root progression (excluding the two-part section) interval structure, and dissonance. Bracket and identify each cadence.

Alma Redemptoris Mater

4. Write a *homophonic* setting in three voices employing the indicated harmonies and rhythms. Then write a version with more interesting lines, containing passing tones and escape tones and often ignoring the indicated rhythm.

# 6

# Mid 15th Century Polyphony

1. Below is given a portion of a paraphrase Mass by Dufay, *Missa Ave Regina Caelorum.* The tenor (the paraphrase line) is given as Dufay wrote it, along with the basic chordal structure. Finish the movement with the other three voices in the style of the opening measures. Note where cadences and suspensions are indicated. Pass - ing tones and escape tones can also be used.

(cadence with 4-3 susp.)

e⁶₃    G⁵₃    e⁶₃    F⁵₃    G⁵₃    e⁶₃    a⁵₃    F⁵₃    d⁵₃    C⁶₃    d⁵₃  .  C⁵₃    G⁵₃    C⁸₅

2. Analyze the following fifteenth century chanson for
   • cadence (identify type and tone level)
   • dissonance (circle and identify)
   • chord and interval structure

fem - me    Qui    est    tout ————— cler    que ———

c'est ———— la    da - ————— me    Qui ———

de ——— nulle    au - tre — n'est — pas - sé - e.

3. Write the cadences described below.

Double-leading-tone cadence with an under-third, on G

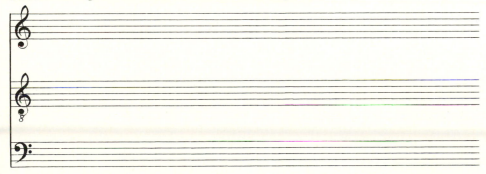

Double-leading-tone cadence with a 7–6 suspension, on F

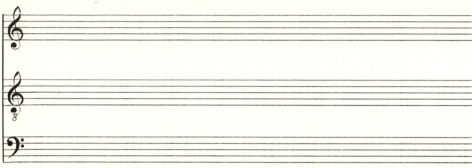

V–I cadence with an octave leap, on C

Single-leading-tone cadence with a 7–6 suspension, on d

V–I cadence with a 4–3 suspension, on G

Double-leading-tone cadence with a 4–3 and a 7–6 suspension, on d

V–I cadence with a 4–3 suspension and an under–third, on G

V–I cadence with an octave leap, under–third, and 4–3 suspension, on C

4. Identify the following cadences mentioning any dissonance or unusual feature.

5. Below is given the beginning of a fauxbourdon piece by Gilles Binchois, a contemporary of Dufay. Also given is the chant *Veni, Creator Spiritus*, on which Binchois's top voice is based. Finish the piece. The top line should paraphrase the chant throughout, using additional notes where appropriate. The middle voice in fauxbourdon must always remain a perfect fourth below the top voice. The bottom voice must produce only the intervals of an octave and a sixth below the top voice (but avoid parallel octaves). Cadences should occur at those points in the chant marked by asterisks. As far as possible, try to create interesting lines and rhythms in all voices.

# 7

# Early 16th Century Polyphony

1. Compose passages in four parts, following the indicated harmonic scheme. Try to
   create interesting and rhythmically independent lines.

2. The beginning of an imitative piece is given below. Continue the top two lines in free counterpoint (without imitation) and add the tenor and bass lines on the opening imitation, ending the entire section with a V–I cadence on D.

3. Analyze *Fama Malum* by Josquin.

   a. Label all points of imitation.

   b. Indicate use of augmentation or diminution of material.

   c. Bracket and label all cadences.

   d. Indicate harmonic motion specifically, with all dissonance labelled, from measure 7 to 31.

Fama Malum

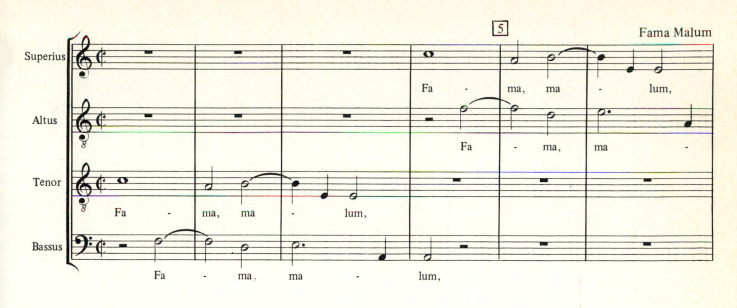

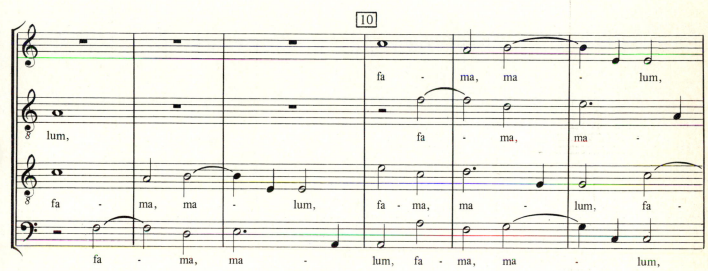

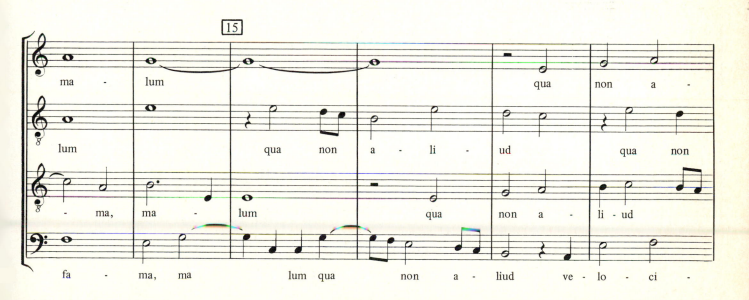

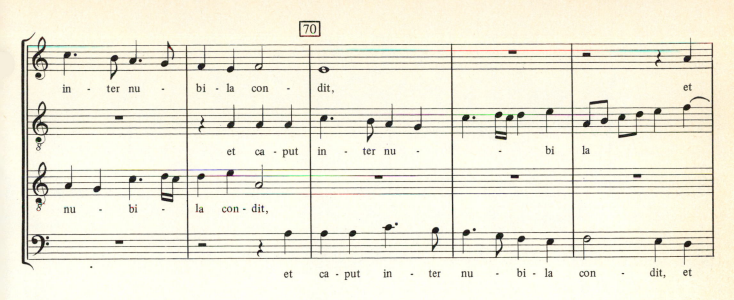

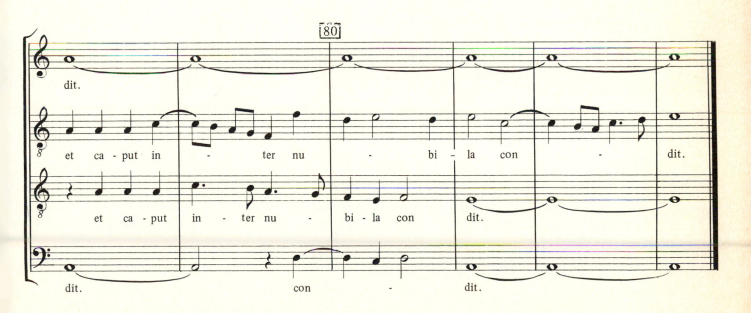

3. Below is the beginning of a canon from the *Missa Pange Lingua* by Josquin. Complete the example with a continuation of the canon in both voices. At the end, break the canon and cadence on A.

4. Construct suspensions as indicated. In the four-part example, add the three upper voices, writing a suspension in one of the parts.

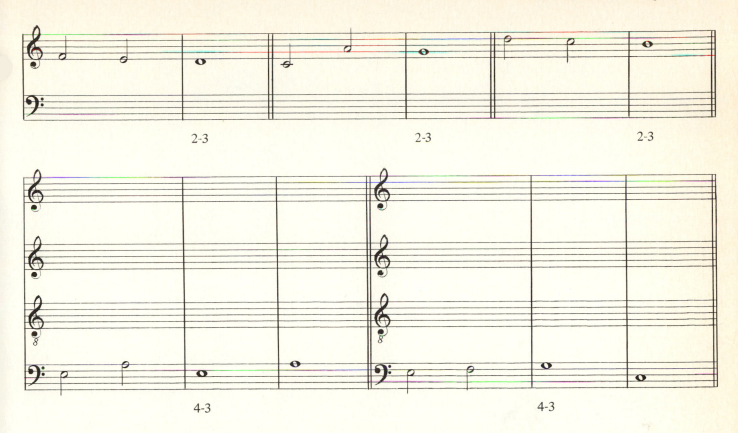

5. Write cadences of the three types indicated, ending on the designated triads. Each should use four voices.

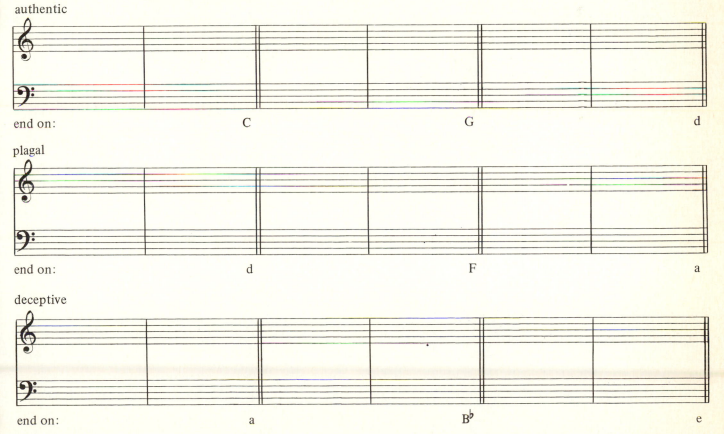

# 8

# Late 16th Century Polyphony

 . 1. Compose the following examples in four parts, using homophonic texture. Try to create interesting lines within the homophonic framework.

a.

$g_3^5$   $A_3^5$   $d_3^5$   $g_3^5$   $e^o{}_3^6$   $F_3^5$   $B^\flat{}_3^5$   $g_3^5$   $D_3^6$   $g_3^5$   $D_3^5$   $G_3^5$
(9-8sus) (4-3sus)

b.

$F_3^5$  $F_3^5$  $d$   $C_3^6$  $F_3^5$  $B^\flat{}_3^5$   $B^\flat{}_3^5$  $g_3^5$  $D_3^6$  $g_3^5$  $d_3^5$  $C_3^6$  $F_3^5$  $B^\flat{}_3^5$   $C_3^5$   $F_3^5$
                                                                                            (4-3sus)
                                                       (9-8sus)        passing 7th

2. Construct cambiatas or suspensions as indicated, using four voices and the given harmonic progressions.

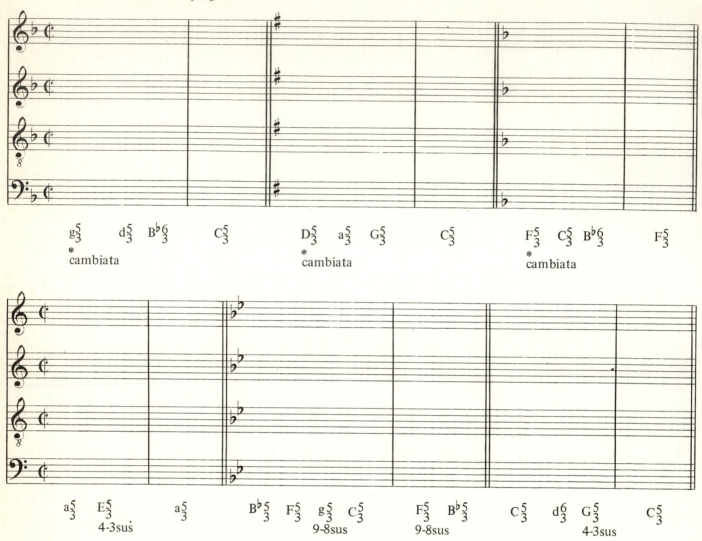

$g_3^5$    $d_3^5$  $B\flat_3^6$    $C_3^5$          $D_3^5$   $a_3^5$  $G_3^5$        $C_3^5$        $F_3^5$  $C_3^5$  $B\flat_3^6$      $F_3^5$

*cambiata                          *cambiata                      *cambiata

$a_3^5$  $E_3^5$        $a_3^5$        $B\flat_3^5$  $F_3^5$  $g_3^5$  $C_3^5$      $F_3^5$  $B\flat_3^5$      $C_3^5$  $d_3^6$  $G_3^5$        $C_3^5$

4-3sus                          9-8sus              9-8sus                      4-3sus

3.  Write the following cadences as indicated.

Authentic, with passing 7th on the V chord

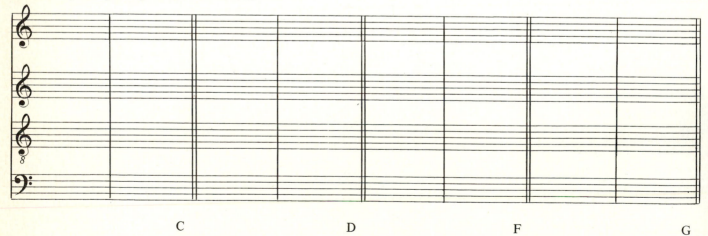

C                    D                    F                    G

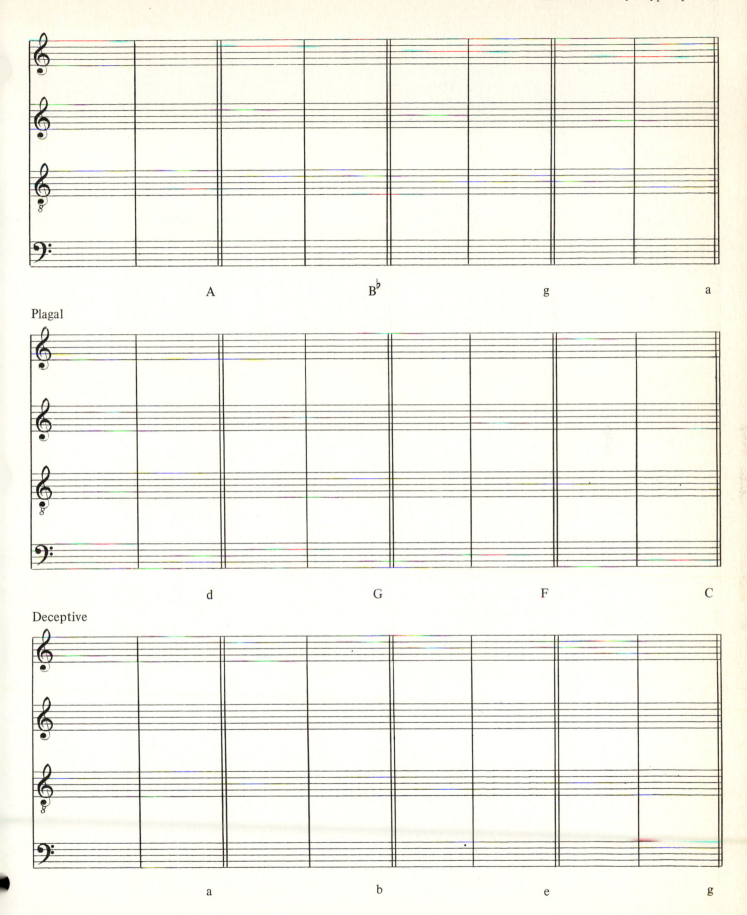

4. For the following motet, *Super flúmina Babilónis* by Palestrina, analyze the points of imitation throughout. In addition, briefly answer the questions below:

a. What two tonal levels are primarily emphasized throughout the piece? Explain the reasons for your choices.

b. Bracket the beginning of each imitation and indicate the voice in which it is imitated. Be careful to look for two voices which are imitated.

c. Is there continual imitation, or are there breaks in the texture when chordal texture is predominant? Give examples.

d. Explain the cadence in measures 46–47.

e. Explain the final cadence. Does it have a historical precedent?

f.  What is the predominant root movement used in the piece? What is it at the major cadence points?

g.  What types of dissonances are employed in the piece? Is there one dissonance that seems to be more prominent than others, especially at cadences?

Super flúmina Babilónis

# General Review: Chapters 5–8

I. Briefly answer the following questions.

1. The three characteristic cadences found in the early fifteenth century are _____ , _____ , and _____ .

2. What is the process of modifying a chant line for use in a polyphonic piece? _____

3. A texture which is primarily chordal, with the voices generally moving together, is called _____ .

4. What is the name for a dissonance which is approached by step and left by leap? _____

5. What is the primary dissonance which is *prepared*? _____

6. The name for a shift of a normal metric accent is _____ .

7. What are the three rhythmic stages of a suspension? _____ , _____ and _____

8. Two suspensions occurring simultaneously are referred to as a _____ .

9. The modified modal cadence uses what kind of triadic/intervallic structure? _____ to _____

10. In the tonal (authentic) cadence, the first chord is in _____ position.

11. A melody performed backwords is described as being in _____ .

12. A piece for two notated voices, in which a third voice always doubles the top one at the perfect fourth below, is called _____ .

13. What do we call the speed of change in the root movement of a piece? _____

14. A V–I cadence where the lowest voice skips up an octave and the middle voice becomes the bass is called an _____ _____ cadence.

15. What are the primary cadences used by Dufay? _____ , _____

16. If the leading tone at a cadence moves down a step and then skips up to the tonic, it is called an _____ _____ .

17. What is the process by which a composer divides the rhythmic values of a line by one-half or one-third? _____

18. In cantus–firmus technique, which voice uses the borrowed melody? _____

19. Name a famous fifteenth–century secular melody which was used as a cantus firmus in numerous pieces. _____ _____

20. The technique of repeating one vocal line, completely, in another voice is called _____ .

21. If a melodic fragment is immediately repeated in the same voice at a different pitch level, the technique is called _____ .

22. If a fragment of a voice is immediately repeated in subsequent voices, it is called _____ .

23. A cadence with the root movement of a perfect fourth down is called _____ .

24. A cadence with the root movement of a perfect fifth down is called _____ .

25. What is a cadence with the root movement of a second up called? _____

26. A 2–3 suspension is usually called a _____ _____ .

27. If a piece employs a V–I cadence to a scale degree other than the tonic of the piece, what is it called? _____ _____

28. The interval of three whole tones is called a _____ .

29. What two special resolutions of suspensions are found in the late Renaissance? _____ and _____

30. The borrowing of two or more lines from an existing composition to serve as the basis for a new work is called _____ .

II. Answer the following questions in discursive style, using the space provided.

1. Compare the basic traits of Dunstable to those of Palestrina.

melody

harmony

cadences

dissonance

rhythm

texture

techniques

2. Describe in detail the cadences employed by Dunstable, Dufay, Josquin, and Palestrina. Indicate which composer(s) used which cadence, and the basic frequency of use by that composer.

3. What kinds of dissonance were used in the Renaissance? Provide a detailed account of each type and its use.

# 9

# Early 17th Century Harmonic Practice

1. Complete the following figured--bass pattern, using four voices in a homophonic setting.

*adapted from Sant' Alessio by Landi*

2. Complete the keyboard realization of the following figured bass. The texture may vary from two to four voices as desired. Indicate each use of a secondary dominant.

*adapted from Vittori*

3. Complete the following dominant–seventh chords in four voices, providing the proper resolution of each. (Capital letters refer to major keys, lower case letters to minor keys.)

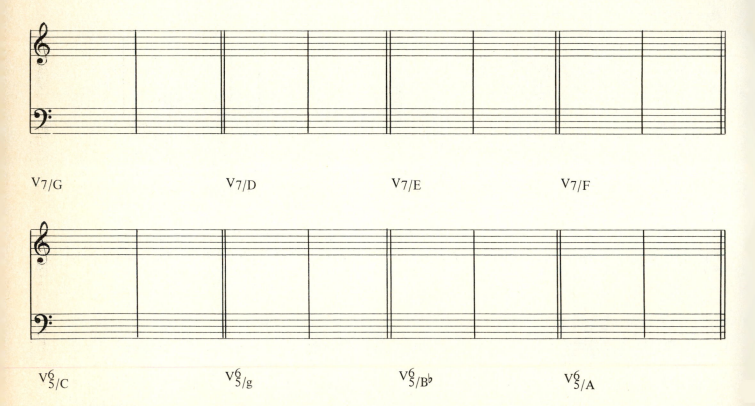

$V_7/G$ $\qquad$ $V_7/D$ $\qquad$ $V_7/E$ $\qquad$ $V_7/F$

$V^6_5/C$ $\qquad$ $V^6_5/g$ $\qquad$ $V^6_5/B\flat$ $\qquad$ $V^6_5/A$

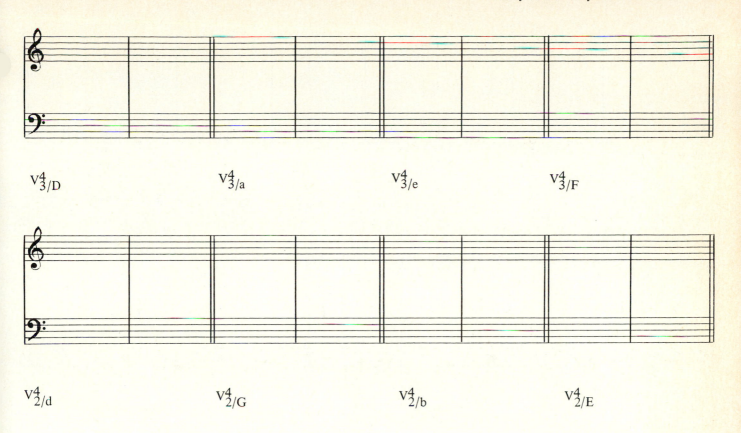

$V^4_3/D$           $V^4_3/a$           $V^4_3/e$           $V^4_3/F$

$V^4_2/d$           $V^4_2/G$           $V^4_2/b$           $V^4_2/E$

4. Write the following chord progressions in four voices using proper voice leading.

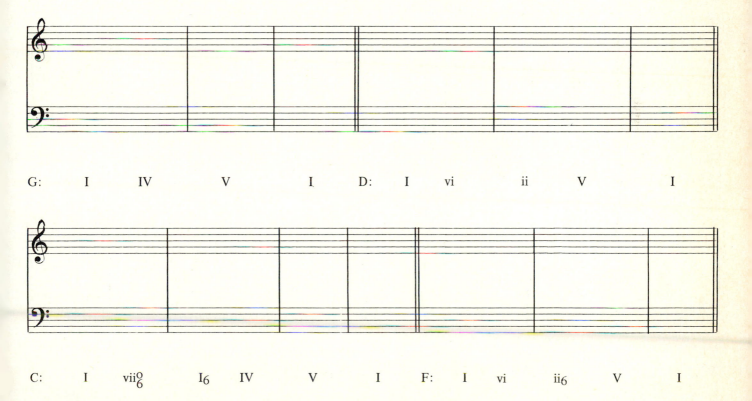

G:    I    IV    V    I    D:  I    vi    ii    V    I

C:    I    vii°$_6$    I$_6$    IV    V    I    F:  I    vi    ii$_6$    V    I

A:    I    IV    V    vi    I$^6_4$    V$_7$    I    G:    I    vi    ii$_6$    IV    I$^6_4$    V$_7$    I

F:    I    vi    V$_7$/V    V    I

C:    I    vi    IV    V$^6_5$/V    V    V$^6_5$/vi    vi    ii$_6$    I$^6_4$    V$_7$    I

G:    I    V$_7$    I    vi    V$^6_5$/vi    vi    IV    ii    V$^6_5$/V    V    I
                                                                              8 − 7

5. Provide a Roman-numeral analysis of the following monody by Caccini. Indicate all secondary dominants, including those not employing a seventh as part of the chord.

Fillide mia

Fil - li - de mi - a, ___ se di bel - tà sei va - ga,

D'o - gn'al - tra cu - ra o mai ___ di - sgom - br'il co -

re, ___ Ar - di d'a - mo - re! ___ Ar -

di d'a - mo - re! Ar - di d'a - mo - re! ___

# 10

# Mid 17th Century Harmony

1. Provide inner voices for the chorales given below. Be careful to avoid parallel octaves and fifths between any two parts.

a.

adapted from J. H. Schein

b.

adapted from J. H. Schein

2. In the following, alter the bass line to make it more musical. Use chordal inversions; add passing tones; add altered pitches in order to create chords of secondary function or to effect modulations.

3. Complete the following chorale in three stages. First, add a bass line constructed solely of roots of appropriate harmonies.
   a. Second, alter the bass line to avoid parallelisms and to create a melodic flow.
   b. You may wish to include tones from chords of secondary function. Finally, add the inner voices.

4. The following chorale contains numerous mistakes. Find and circle them. Work out a proper solution on the staves provided. You may change the progression in order to solve the problem, but the soprano line must not be altered.

5. Analyze harmonically the following keyboard piece by the seventeenth-century
French composer Chambonnières.

Sarabande

# 11

# Late 17th Century Harmony

1. Realize the following figured–bass patterns in four voices. Provide harmonic analyses.

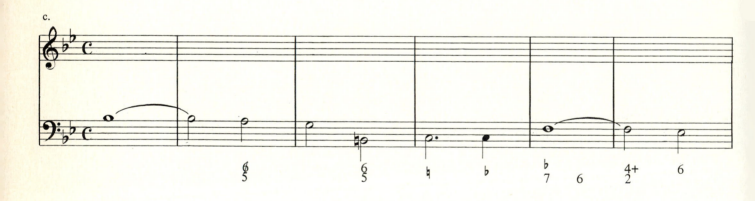

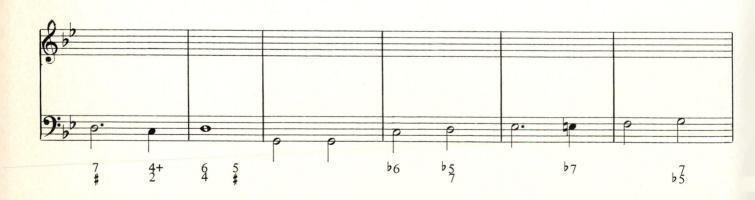

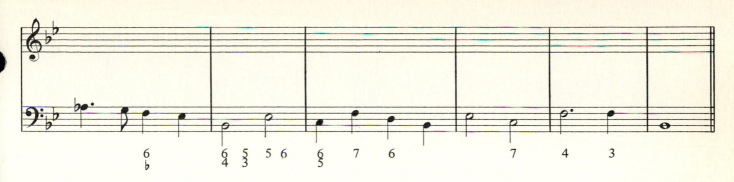

2. Write the following chords in four voices as indicated, with their proper resolutions.

D:  $V_7/V$                E♭: $V_7/ii$                E: $V_7/IV$                F: $V_7/vi$

g: $V^6_5/III$                d: $V^4_3/VI$                c: $V^4_2/V$                f: $V^6_5/iv$

e: $vii°_7$                f: $vii°_7$                g: $vii°_7/V$                B♭: $vii°_7/ii$

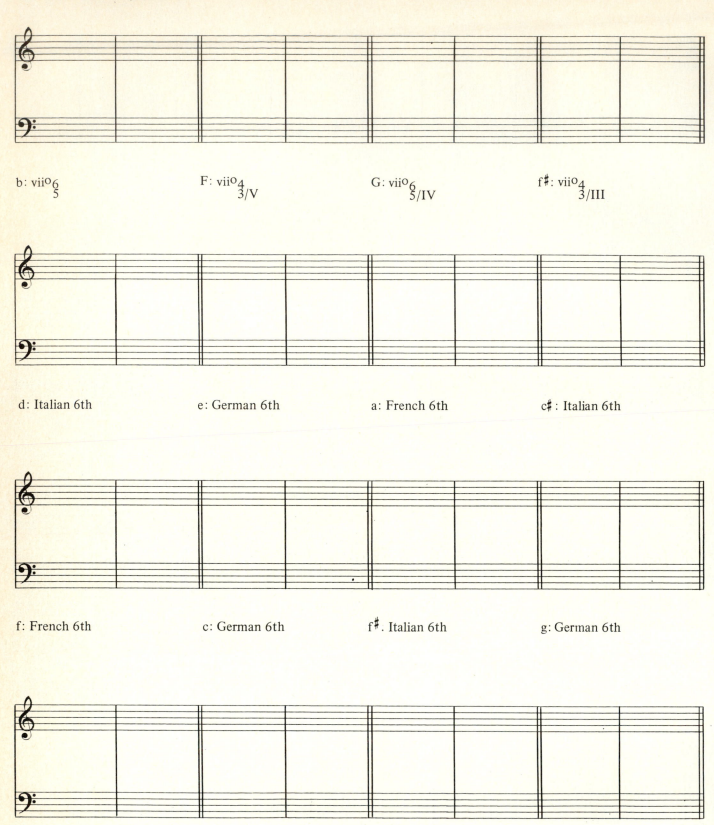

b: vii°$^6_5$                F: vii°$^4_3$/V                G: vii°$^6_5$/IV                f#: vii°$^4_3$/III

d: Italian 6th                e: German 6th                a: French 6th                c#: Italian 6th

f: French 6th                c: German 6th                f#. Italian 6th                g: German 6th

d: ii∅$^7$                e: ii∅$^6_5$                a: ii∅$^6_5$                b: ii∅$^7$

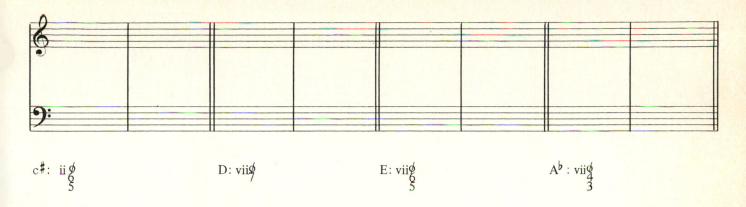

c#: ii∅$\frac{6}{5}$          D: vii∅7          E: vii∅$\frac{6}{5}$          A♭: vii∅$\frac{4}{3}$

3. Provide an analysis of the following chords as they function within the indicated keys. Then resolve each chord properly.

g:                    B:                              d:                    c:

4. Complete the following progressions in four voices as indicated.

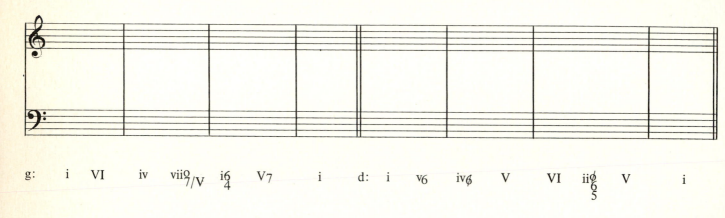

g:    i    VI    iv    vii⁰7/V    i6/4    V7    i    d:    i    v6    iv6    V    VI    iiø6/5    V    i

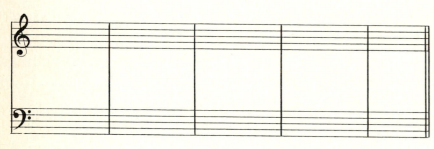

B♭:    I    V6/5/ii    ii    I6    IV    V6/5/V    I6/4    V    I

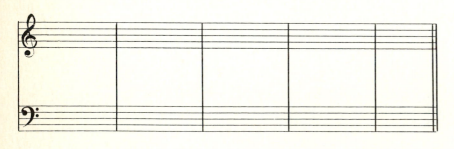

e:    i    v6    iv6    V    i    iiø6/5    i6/4    V7    i

D:    I    vi    IV    V    vi    ii    V    I    vii°$_{7}$/ii    V$_{7}$/V    V$_{7}$    I

c:    i    v6    iv6    iv$^{6}_{5}$    i$^{6}_{4}$    V    VI    iv    vii°$_{7}$/V    V$_{7}$    i

d:    i    vii°$_{7}$/ii    vii°$_{7}$/III    III    vii°$_{7}$/iv    iv    ii$^{6}_{4}$$_{3}$    V    i

5. Harmonically analyze the following movement from a trio sonata by Purcell. Then discuss the use of phrase structure, cadences, and chromaticism, and the use of motives in the violin and bass viol parts.

Violin

Bass Viol

Organ

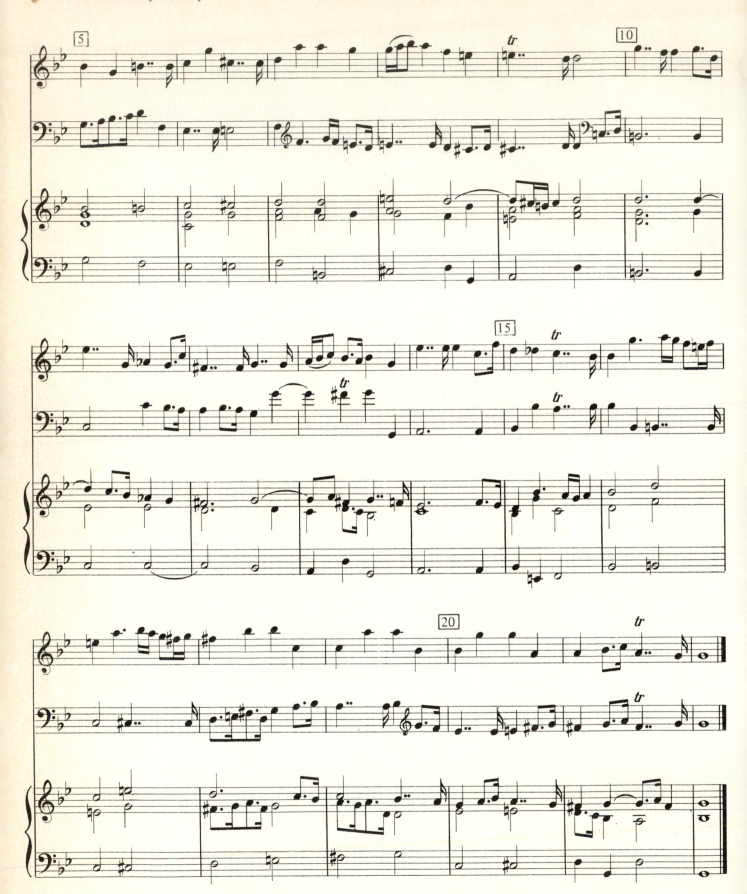

phrase structure:

cadences:

chromaticism:

motives used:

# 12

# Early 18th Century Harmony

1. Complete the following figured–bass example. Include an analysis as well.

from *Concerto Grosso*, Op. 6, No. 4, by Corelli

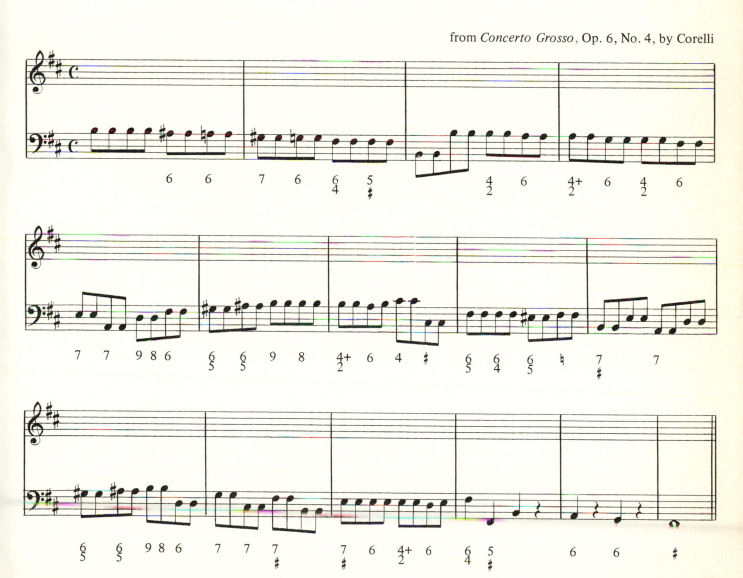

2. Harmonically analyze the following Concerto Grosso by Corelli.

*Concerto Grosso*, Op. 6, No. 3

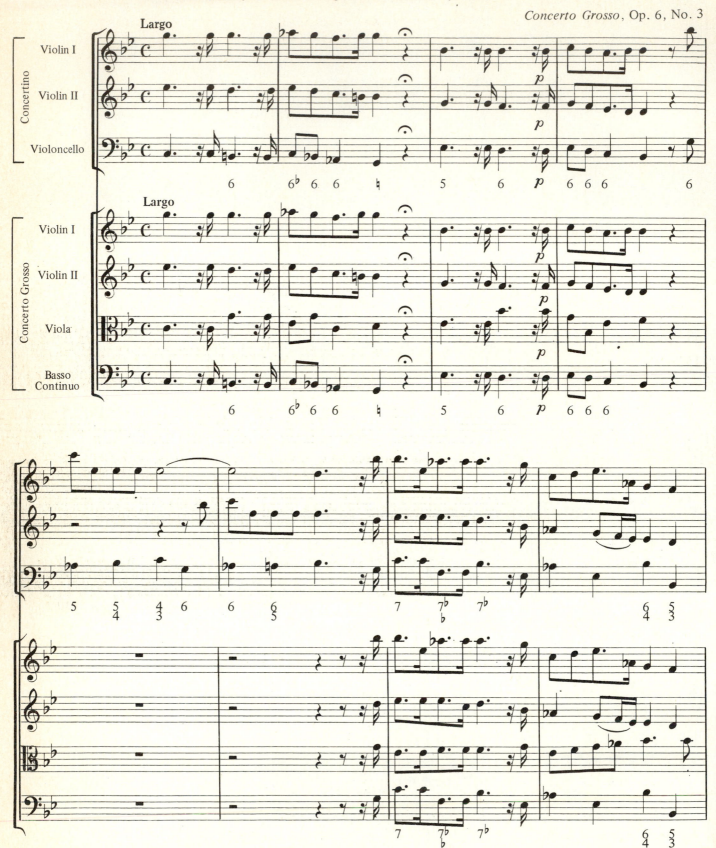

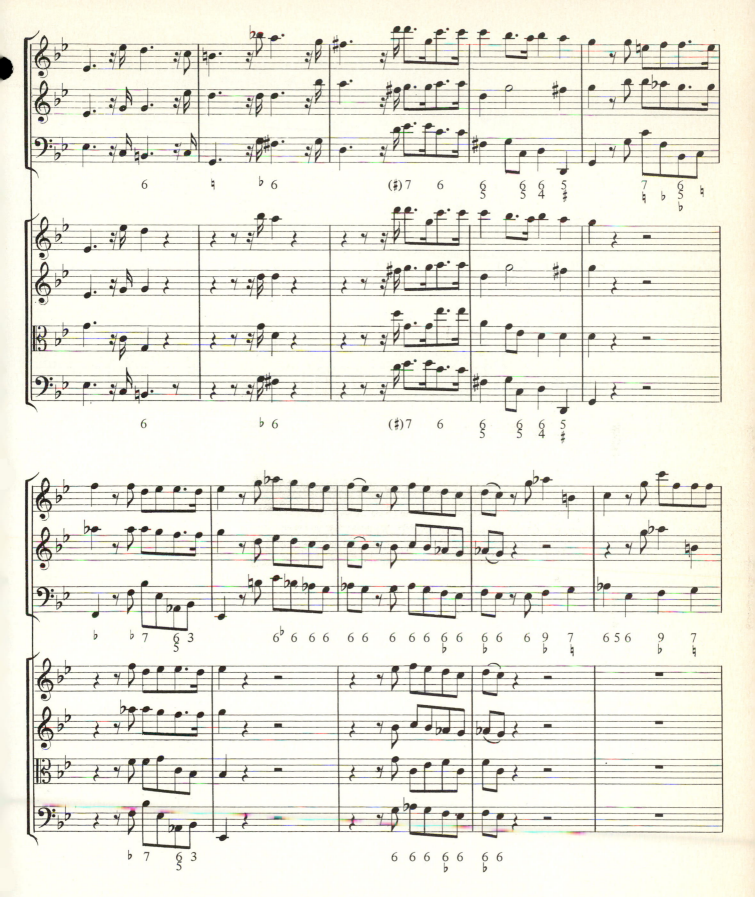

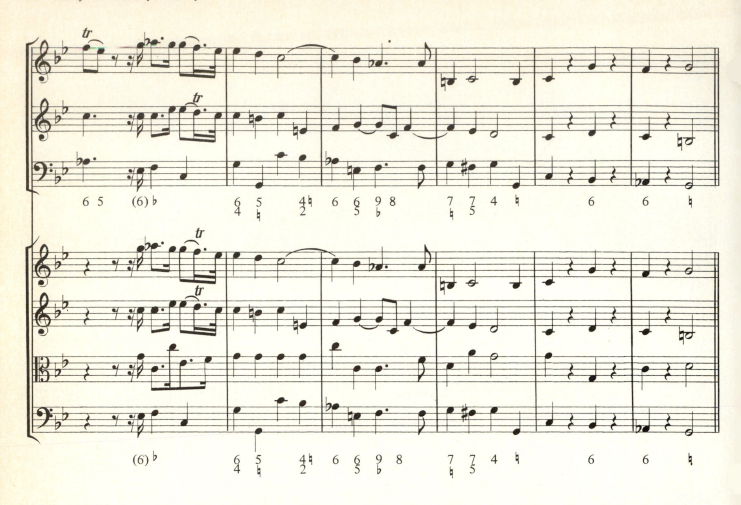

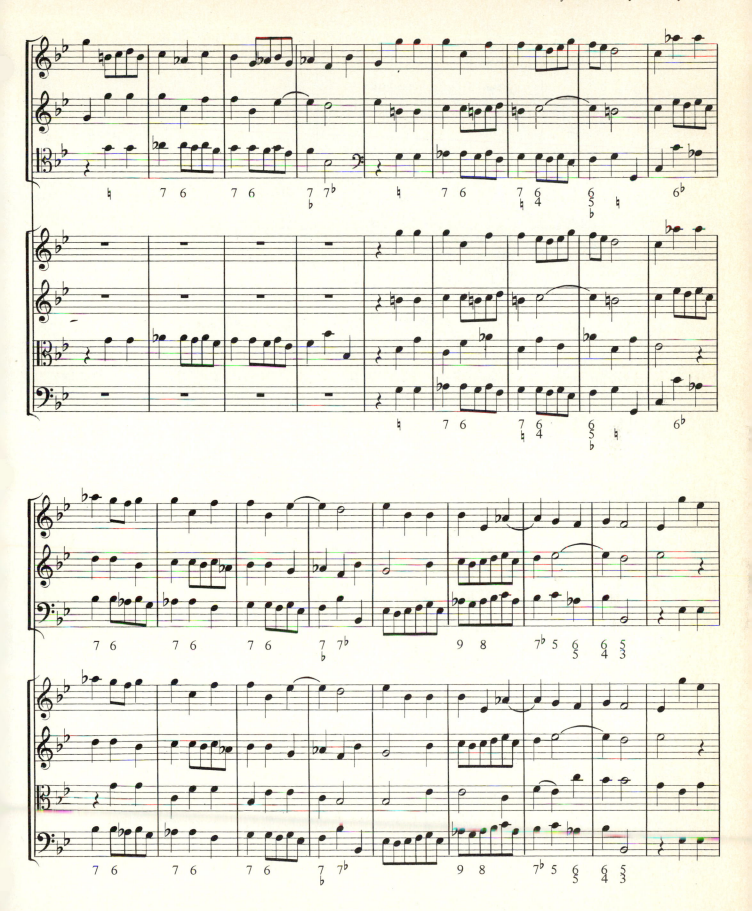

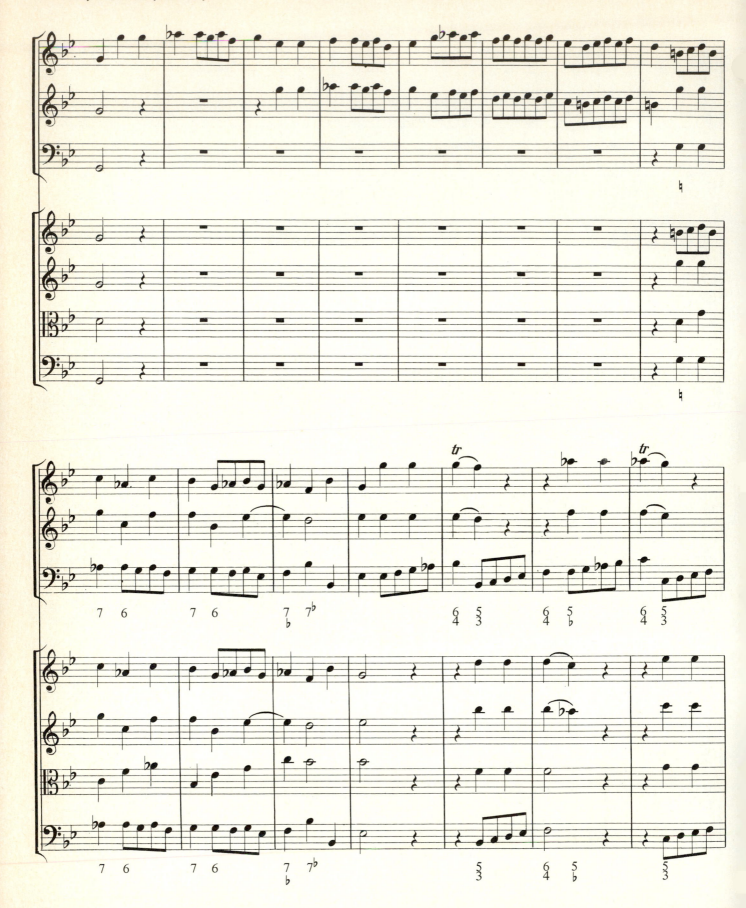

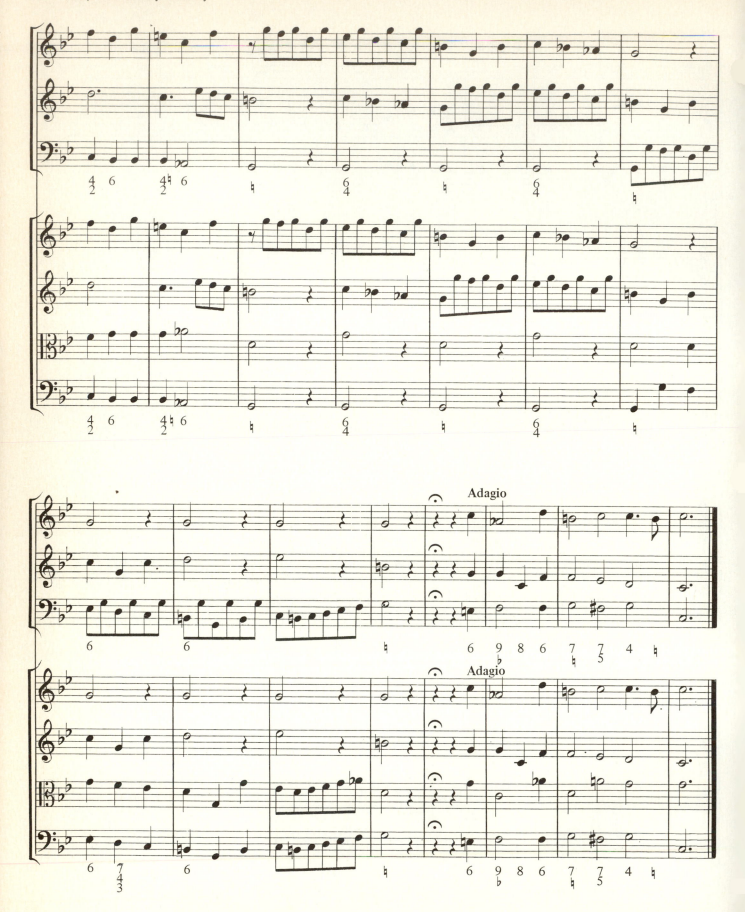

3.  Write the following chords with their proper resolutions.

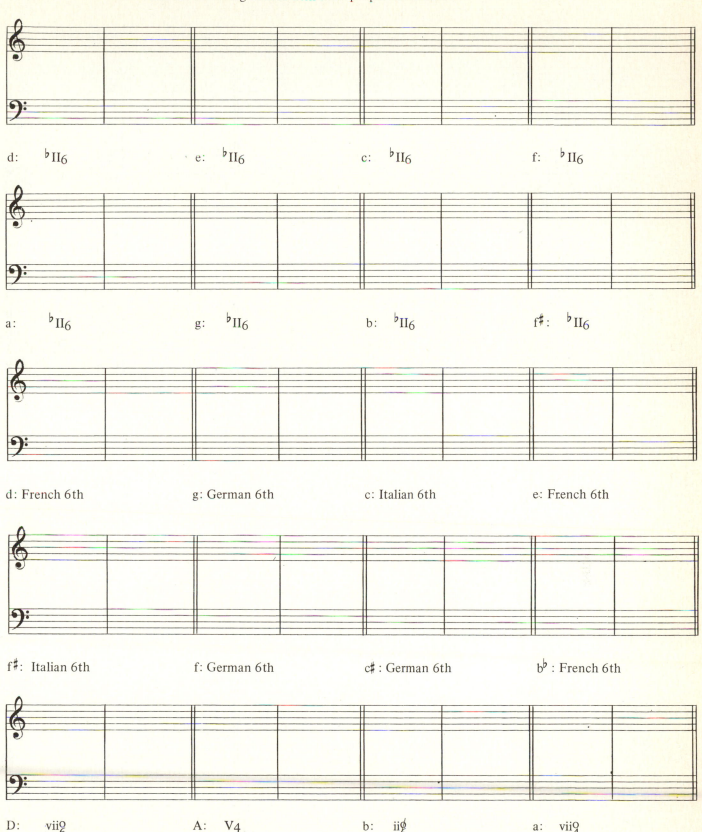

d:  $^\flat$II$_6$          e:  $^\flat$II$_6$          c:  $^\flat$II$_6$          f:  $^\flat$II$_6$

a:  $^\flat$II$_6$          g:  $^\flat$II$_6$          b:  $^\flat$II$_6$          f$^\sharp$:  $^\flat$II$_6$

d: French 6th          g: German 6th          c: Italian 6th          e: French 6th

f$^\sharp$:  Italian 6th          f: German 6th          c$^\sharp$ : German 6th          b$^\flat$ : French 6th

D:  vii$^o{}_6^6$$_{5}$/iii          A:  V$^4_2$/V          b:  ii$^{\o}_6^6${}_5          a:  vii$^o{}_4^4${}_3/VI

5.  Write the following cadences in four-voice texture.

authentic

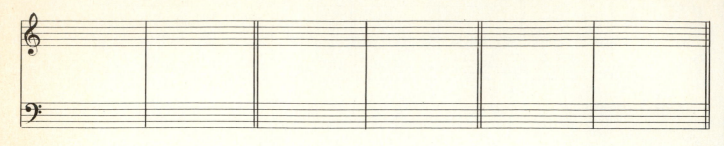

c#:                          d:                          b♭:

plagal

f:                          B♭:                          b:

deceptive

A:                          F#:                          g:

Phrygian

g:                          c:                          f:

# 13

# Mid 18th Century Harmony

1. Harmonically analyze the following recitatives from Bach's cantatas. Be careful to indicate precisely where modulations occur, with pivot chords clearly marked.

a. *from Wo soll ich fliehen hin*

Meer, da - hin ich mei - ne Sün - den sen - ke, und wenn ich mich zu

6        6     5

die - sem Stro - me len - ke, so macht er mich von mei - nen Fle - cken leer.

7♭   ∅      ∅   6       6♭   5      6   5
5                 5                            4   ♯

*from Wie schön leuchtet der Morgenstern*

b.

Basso

Ein ird-'scher Glanz, ein leib-lich Licht, rührt mei-ne See-le nicht; ein Freu - - denschein ist

Continuo

mir von Gott ent-stan-den, denn ein voll-ko-mmnes Gut, des Hei-lands Leib und Blut, ist

zur Er-quick-ung da. So muss uns ja der ü-ber-rei-che Se-gen, der uns von E-wig-keit be-

stimmt,    und un - ser Glau - be    zu    sich    nimmt,    zum Dank und Preis    be - we - gen.

c.

from *Wo soll ich fliehen hin*

Soprano

Continuo

Ich bin ja    nur    das klein-ste Theil der Welt,    und    da des Blu-tes ed-ler Saft    un-

end - lich gros - se    Kraft be - währt er - hält,    dass je - der Tro - pfen,    so    auch    noch    so

klein,    die gan - ze Welt kann    rein von Sün-den ma-chen,    so    lass dein Blut    ja nicht an mir ver-

der - ben,    es kom - me mir zu    gut,    dass ich den Him - mel kann er - er - ben.

from *Es ist das Heil uns kommen her*

Gott gab uns ein Ge-setz doch wa-ren wir zu schwach, dass wir es hät-ten halt-ten

kön-nen; wir gin-gen nur den Sün-den nach, kein Mensch war fromm zu nen-nen; der

Geist bleib an dem Fleische kle-ben und wag-te nicht zu wi-der-stre-ben. Wir Soll-ten in Ge-set-ze

gehn, und dort als wie in ei-nem Spie-gel sehn, wie un-se-re Na-tur un-ar-tig

sei: und den-noch blei-ben wir da-bei; aus eig-ner Kraft war Nie-mand fä-hig der Sün-den

Un-art zu ver-la-ssen, er möcht' auch al-le Kraft zu-sam-men-fas-sen.

Provide a keyboard realization below for the first Bach example.

2.  Harmonize the following chorale melodies in four voices in the manner indicated.

a.  Following the progressions indicated, complete these chorales.

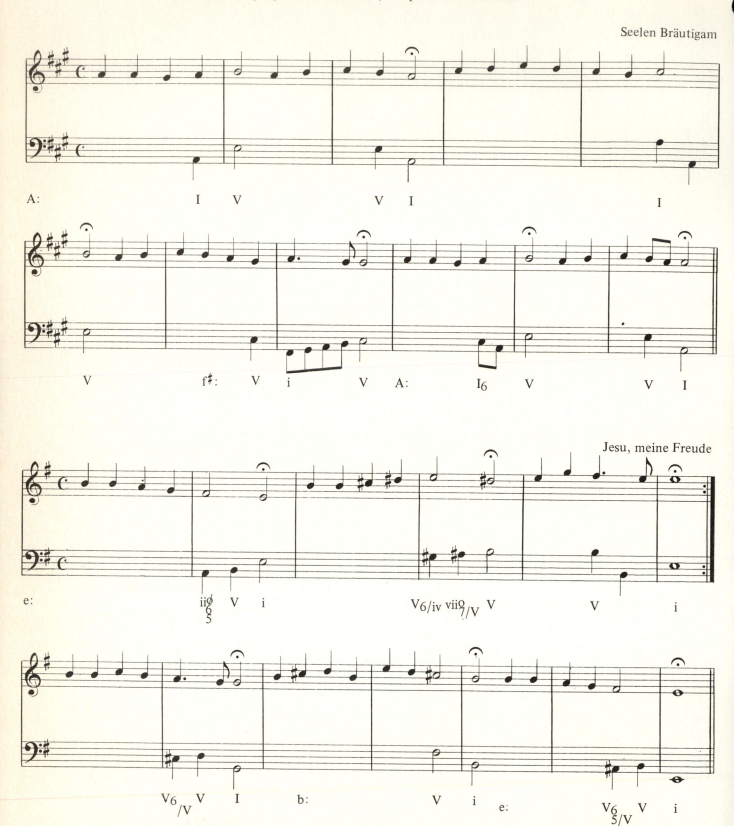

Seelen Bräutigam

Jesu, meine Freude

b. Harmonize in four parts, incorporating the modulations indicated. Establish each
   key with a strong cadential progression.

Gott der Vater wohn' uns bei

D Major:                                    modulate to b minor        modulate to A Major

modulate to D Major

Durch Adams Fall ist ganz verderbt

d minor:                                    modulate to a minor

modulate to F Major               modulate to G Major          modulate to a minor

c. In the following chorale several altered chords have been indicated. Some of these chords indicate modulations, and some are simply embellishing chords (secondary dominants, augmented-sixth chords, and the like). Complete the chorale in four voices. Be careful to use voice leading that introduces these chords smoothly.

Vater unser im Himmelreich

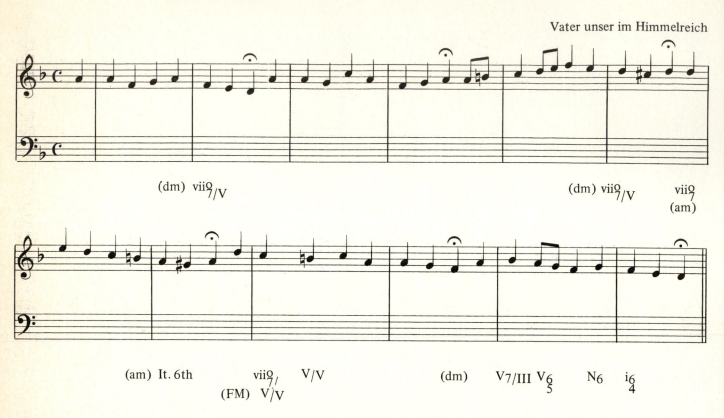

(dm) vii°₇/V                    (dm) vii°₇/V        vii°₇
                                                   (am)

(am) It. 6th              vii°₇/         V/V        (dm)    V₇/III  V₆₅    N₆    i₆₄
                  (FM)  V/V

d. Analyze the following chorale to determine its modulatory areas. Complete the chorale in four voices, using several secondary dominant chords, at least one augmented-sixth chord or Neapolitan-sixth chord, and suspensions at the cadence, as well as passing tones and neighboring tones.

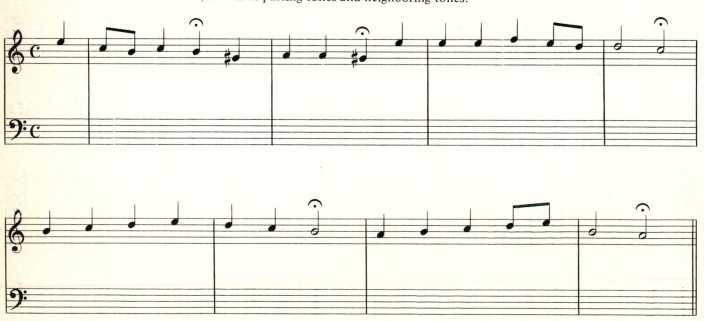

3. With the fugue subjects provided, write an exposition to a fugue. Bring in each voice at the appropriate time and in the proper key, while continuing the other voices in free counterpoint. Cadence after all four voices have entered.

a.

b.

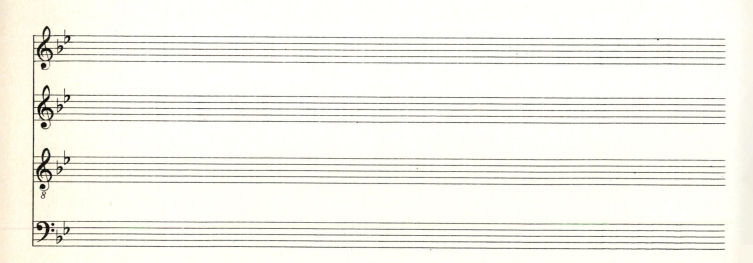

# General Review: Chapters 9–13

I. Briefly answer the following questions.

1. A Baroque composition employing a constantly repeated bass line is called a _____.

2. The bass line of such a piece is called a _____ _____.

3. A $I_6^4$ chord appearing on a strong beat and resolving to a V chord is a _____ _____ $I_6^4$.

4. A dominant chord emphasizing a level other than the primary tonic is called a _____ _____.

5. The shorthand system used in the Baroque period for notating harmonic progressions is called _____ _____.

6. How do you notate a raised sixth above the bass in this system? _____

7. How do you indicate a lowered third? _____

8. What chords are major in a major key? ____ ____ ____

9. What chords are minor in a major key? ____ ____ ____

10. What chord is diminished in a major key? _____

11. What chords are major in a minor key? ____ ____ ____

12. What chords are minor in a minor key? ____ ____

13. What chords are diminished in a minor key? ____ ____

14. What is the name of the third scale degree? _____ fourth scale degree? _____.

15. Diminished fifths generally resolve _____ ; augmented fourths usually resolve _____ .

16. The seventh of a $V_7$ chord always resolves _____ .

17. When in the course of a composition the key changes to another key whose tonic is contained in the original scale, the process is called _____ _____.

18. Primary function in the diatonic scale is represented by a basic chord progression of _____ _____ _____ _____ _____.

19. A reversal of the normal functional progression is called _____ .

20. A chordal texture is called _____ .

21. What is the term for the chord that functions in both keys at the point where a modulation occurs? _____ _____

22. What cadence moves V–vi? _____

23. What cadence ends on V? _____

24. Which note of the scale do you never double in a four-part setting? _____

25. A $iv_6$ is called an _____ _____.

   $iv_5^6$? _____ _____.

   $ii_4^6{}_3$? _____ _____.

26. Give the Roman–numeral symbols for the following cadences:

     authentic _____   _____

     plagal _____   _____

     deceptive _____   _____

     half _____   _____

     Phrygian _____   _____

27. What intervals are contained above the root in a diminished–seventh chord?

     _____   _____   _____

28. A diminished triad with a minor seventh is a _____   _____.

29. Which chord is half diminished naturally in the major scale? _____
    minor scale? _____

30. The root of a fully diminished seventh is always a _____ step below the
    resolution pitch.

31. Which chords can be major/minor seventh chords? _____

32. Which chords can be diminished/diminished seventh chords? _____

33. Which chords can be major/major seventh chords? _____

34. The augmented-sixth chord is derived from a _____ passing tone.

35. A major chord built on the lowered second scale degree is a _____
    _____.

36. ‖: A :‖: B A :‖  is called _____   _____.

37. What is the term for the repetition of a chord pattern at a different level?

     _____   _____.

38. A Baroque solo sonata contains a solo line and a _____ part.

39. A metric shift emphasizing two–beat groupings in a triple meter or three–beat
    groupings in a duple is called _____.

40. iv$_6$–V in a minor key is called a _____   _____.

41. The counterpoint to a subject in a fugue is called a _____   _____.

42. What is a piling–up of voices in a fugue called? _____

43. The second statement of the fugue subject is the _____ .

44. The second statement can be either _____ or _____ .

45. A piece containing only one theme or subject is called _____ .

46. The form AAB is called _____   _____ .

47. What is the first section of a fugue called? _____

48. Give the typical arrangement of dances in an eighteenth–century suite.

     _____, _____, _____, _____, _____

49. What is the middle section of the fugue, in which development takes place?

     _____.

II. Answer the following questions in discursive style, using the space provided.

    1. Discuss the use and development of dissonance from Monteverdi to Bach. What dissonances were employed, how were they treated, how did they change, and what·was the amount of dissonance in each period?

    2. Define as completely as possible the stylistic characteristics of a Bach chorale. Consider melodic lines in all voices, harmonic use, rhythm, form(s), voice leading and chordal structure, modulatory possibilities, chordal alterations and so on.

    3. What are some of the differences in harmonic usage between the major and the minor mode? Suggest possible reasons for this.

III. Identify the appropriate material as indicated.

1. Label all the dissonant pitches in the following excerpt.

J. S. Bach

2. Identify the function of each of the following chords within the indicated key.
key.

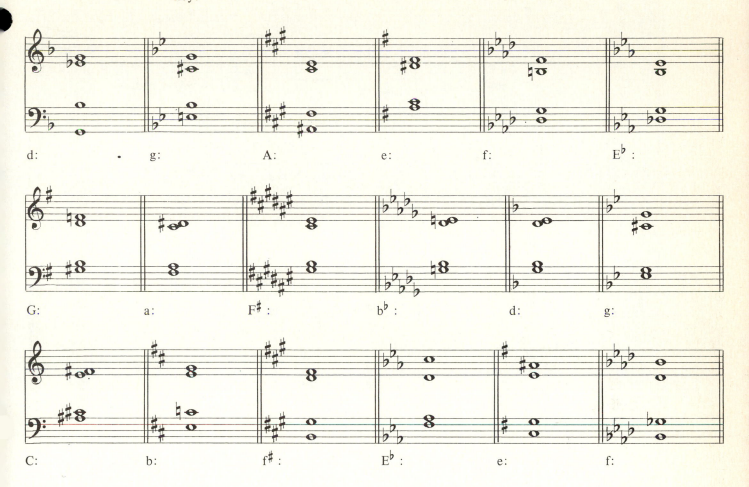

d:          g:          A:          e:          f:          E♭ :

G:          a:          F# :          b♭ :          d:          g:

C:          b:          f# :          E♭ :          e:          f:

3. Study each of the short excerpts below and identify the type of piece that it is
taken from (dance suite, chorale, fugue, passacaglia, trio sonata, solo sonata, solo
song, etc.). Give the approximate date of composition and a possible composer.

a.

[Moderato]

Bass

Ich    lie - ge    und    schla    -          fe,

type: _____

composer/date: _____

b.

Violin

Violin

Continuo

type: _____

composer/date: _____

c.

type: _____

composer/date: _____

d.    **Gigue**

type: _____

composer/date: _____

e.    **Allegro**

Violin

Continuo

type: _____

composer/date: _____

f.

S. Mit Freu - den fahr ich hin zu Gott, ver - lass die Ei - tel - keit;
es ist doch nichts denn Müh und Not in die - ser Sterb - lich - keit.

A. Mit Freu - den fahr ich hin zu Gott, ver - lass die Ei - tel - keit;
es ist doch nichts denn Müh und Not in die - ser Sterb - lich - keit.

T. Mit Freu - den fahr ich hin zu Gott, ver - lass die Ei - tel - keit;
es ist doch nichts denn Müh und Not in die - ser Sterb - lich - keit.

B. Mit Freu - den fahr ich hin zu Gott, ver - lass die Ei - tel - keit;
es ist doch nichts denn Müh und Not in die - ser Sterb - lich - keit.

type: _____

composer/date: _____

g.

[Freely: recitando]

O _____ quam tu pul - chra es, O _____ quam tu pul - chra

type: _____

composer/date: _____

h.

type: _____

composer/date: _____